A Day with Mica Feldspar

BASED ON A TRUE STORY

NAOMI CLAY HORSE

WESTBOW PRESS®
PRESS
A DIVISION OF THOMAS NELSON
& ZONDERVAN

This book is a work of non-fiction. Unless otherwise noted, the author
and the publisher make no explicit guarantees as to the accuracy
of the information contained in this book and in some cases, names
of people and places have been altered to protect their privacy.

WestBow Press books may be ordered through
booksellers or by contacting:

WestBow Press
A Division of Thomas Nelson & Zondervan
1663 Liberty Drive
Bloomington, IN 47403
www.westbowpress.com
1 (866) 928-1240

ISBN: 978-1-4908-8513-1 (sc)
ISBN: 978-1-4908-8512-4 (e)

Library of Congress Control Number: 2015909846

Print information available on the last page.

WestBow Press rev. date: 06/25/2015

Contents

Mica Feldspar dedicates this book to all the children of the world.

Chapter 1

Baby Puppies

Four little tuffs of fur cuddled close to their Toy French Poodle mom. She was soft and silky. They slept quietly and contentedly beside her. Mom's babies looked like puffs of cotton. There were two boy puppies and two girl puppies. The puppies' eyes twitched and their tiny legs quivered. They yawned and stretched. The puppies dreamed of Mother's warm milk.

The puppies opened their eyes. They tried to walk, but their legs were weak and wobbly. Mother joined them in their pen. They nestled into her belly for nourishment. They whined in puppy talk, "Mommy, Mommy, we are very hungry."

The puppies pushed their tiny paws against her as they suckled. Mother licked them gently to wash them as they fed. Like all mothers know, they needed a bath. She also knew her babies needed food and sleep.

The puppies grew stronger. Mother Poodle felt it was safe to spend longer periods of time away from her babies. She needed quiet time for herself. Her puppies were becoming <u>too</u> playful. They fussed and yelped. They pulled on her long ears and pounced on her puffy tail. One of her sons was particularly curious. He nudged his brother and sisters to play. He nudged Mom, too, if she stayed in the pen. Mom needed her sleep and rest. She was glad to get away.

The puppies had no names. Each one of them would have a family some day. Each family would give its puppy a special name. For now, these puppies were not concerned with names. They were busy romping and chasing each other.

A curious boy puppy was white with tan ears. He had one black brother, a brown sister, and a twin sister who looked just like him. His brother was bigger, but that did not matter. This curious puppy could run faster than his brother. He liked to show off by running like a whirlwind! His big brother could not keep up with him.

One day the puppies' owner scooped them out of their pen and placed them in a cardboard box. The puppies huddled together in a corner. They shivered with fear. What did the box mean? The box was strange and scary, but not for the curious pup. He stretched his hind legs to reach the brim of the box. He sniffed the air. This looked like a new adventure to him.

The cardboard box was carefully placed on the back seat of a car. The curious puppy grew anxious to see what fun this adventure would bring. As the car drove away, the curious pup went from one corner of the box to the other. He sniffed and sniffed but could not see over the top of the box. He could not even reach halfway up the box!

The curious pup stepped on his brother and sisters to reach higher, but the box was too tall. He was too small. The pup sat to listen as his brother and sisters huddled together. He was more curious than he had ever been. There was something outside the box he needed to see. "If I could only see," he whined!

The car stopped moving. There were noises outside the car. The curious pup sat very still in the center of the box to listen to every move that was being made. His head turned and tilted. He heard the clang of pipes.

A tent was being put up by an old highway. A fence was placed around the tent. A green carpet was laid down to soften the ground for tender puppy paws. The curious pup jumped inside the box. He tried to see what was happening outside. He heard many strange sounds. There was the clanking of doggy dishes. He could hear water being poured. He had to find out what the meaning of this was. He jumped faster with excitement.

The dog breeder took the box from the car. The curious pup yelped and whimpered. He wanted to be the first one to find out what was happening.

Suddenly three puppies were gathered out of the cardboard box and placed in the tent. His sisters and brother hovered timidly together in the new pen with green carpet. They did not like the tent. They did not like the green carpet. They were so afraid they forgot that their curious brother was still in the box!

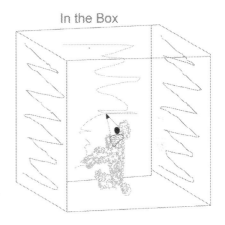

In the Box

Finally the curious puppy was lifted out of the box and placed with his siblings. He sniffed and ran around the pen under the tent. The green carpet was soft under his paws. It was cool inside the tent. Was this a new home?

The curious puppy prompted his brother to play in the big, new house. What an adventure! There was a bowl of fresh water. He pushed his face into it and blew

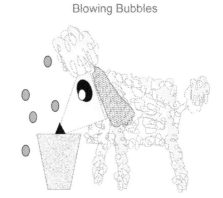

Blowing Bubbles

bubbles. He splashed water on his brother and sisters.

"What fun," he yapped at his brother and sisters. "Let's play. Come on! The water feels great!"

Cars pulled into the parking lot by the old highway. They stopped when people read the sign that said "Puppies for Sale." Human arms reached down and hugged the puppies. They cuddled them, except for one. It was the curious pup. He was too rambunctious. The curious puppy did not understand. He stared at his brother and sisters as they were carried and fondled. He wagged his cotton-ball tail, but no one noticed. His eyes saddened. He wanted a hug too!

The curious puppy did not notice a woman who remained in the tent. She walked around and around. She mumbled something to the owner of the puppies. "How old is he," she asked. The woman watched the curious puppy. Then the owner mumbled something back. She answered, "He is seven weeks old."

The mumbling did not sound exciting. For the first time he would not wag his puffy tail. He sat down cocking his head from side to side. He listened. Was something about to happen? No! The woman got into her truck and drove away. She was gone and someone else took his twin sister away! He was confused. He barked, "Bring my sister back!"

Surprisingly, the curious puppy noticed the woman in the truck returning with green pieces of paper in her hand. Was she coming to play? Was she going to shred paper with him? She gave the green papers to his owner instead! It would have been so much fun shredding paper with her! He was disappointed. The lady did not play, but to his surprise she reached for him! She had bought him with the green pieces of paper. The puppy did not know the green paper was money.

She cuddled him. She snuggled her nose into his soft, silky coat. It was a magical moment. He liked her snuggly nose. He responded to the sound of her beating heart. His puffy, little tail could not stop wagging. The curious puppy squirmed inside her blouse. He rested comfortably. He wondered if she would play peek-a-boo with him. That would be so much fun! He peeked out and then crawled back into her blouse. He was quiet and calm. He liked this new game. This adventure was going to be wonderful fun!

Chapter 2

A Name for Puppy

On the way to the curious puppy's home, his new mom stopped at a clinic. He did not like the place. It smelled like strange dogs, cats and medicine. He did not want to be pulled out of her blouse. His mom said, "Come on, boy. It is okay." The tone of her voice was nice. She handed him to the vet. This did not look like an adventure to him.

The veterinarian probed into his floppy ears and pulled his cyclids wide open. She opened his mouth to look at his teeth and gums. She squeezed his stomach. The vet, Dr. Gage, and his new mom were good friends. Dr. Gage placed the puppy on a scale. He weighed two and a half pounds.

Dr. Gage giggled. She said, "I guess he is all hair! You have a very healthy little boy, Miss Clay Horse. I give Puppy Clay Horse a clean bill of health." The curious puppy looked at his mom. Did he have a name? What was a horse? Was he a horse? Puppy Clay Horse was a very funny name!

Before they went home Miss Clay Horse stuffed him back into her blouse. She stopped to shop for puppy food, doggy dishes, a litter box, and a bag of litter. He was to be an inside dog. There would be no going outside in cold or rainy weather. He was going to be a pampered pet.

The road to the curious puppy's new home seemed very far away. Mom Clay Horse fastened him with her seat belt so he could not wiggle out of her blouse. She did not want him to get hurt. He peeked out from her blouse as she drove. This was a good peeking game! There was so much to see. The new adventure was quiet but lots of fun nonetheless.

He passed farms and ranches. He saw dairy cows and horses. Horses had four legs, two ears and a tail just like him. He was definitely <u>not</u> a horse, but a puppy with a strange name! He did not like the name Puppy Clay Horse.

There was brush land and lots of hills. Suddenly Mom Clay Horse slowed her truck. She turned onto a gravel road. She stopped and stepped out of the truck. She held her precious little cargo inside her blouse to unlock a gate. It was such a big gate. Then they drove onto her driveway.

The yard was huge, too big for a tiny puppy. He would have to stay close to his human mom. He did not want to get lost. He forgot his puppy family in all the excitement but he was still a very curious pup. The puppy was anxious to see what this new adventure would bring.

The house was the biggest house the puppy had ever seen. It was his new home. Upon entering, he saw an elderly woman sitting on a rocking chair. Her hair was white as snow. She was watching television.

His mom took him out of her blouse. Miss Clay Horse mumbled something as she tiptoed behind the old woman. The old woman was Miss Clay Horse's mother. He wished he could understand the mumbling between his mom and his new granny. The best he could do was to watch their gestures. Maybe he would understand that way.

Mom Clay Horse said, "Mother, I brought a surprise for you. It is the same color as the doggy you lost." She handed the puppy to Granny.

"Oh, she is so pretty," the elderly woman said as she held the puppy up in the air to look at it.

"It is a boy, Mother," Mom Clay Horse said.

The elderly woman pushed the puppy away. She handed the puppy back to Mom Clay Horse. She said harshly, "You keep it. I do not want it. I only like girl dogs!"

Mom Clay Horse's heart sank. "Mother, I will train him for you. He is an excellent dog. I watched him carefully and compared him to the other puppies. He will be a very intelligent dog. He will keep you company when I am not here with you."

Puppy's eyes gazed at his mom. He sensed Granny did not like him. He pleaded for help with his eyes. The puppy could not understand. He did not like the way Granny pushed him away. His feelings were hurt. He was sad. He was also glad to be back with his mom. "I should stay away from Granny," he thought. "I like my mom best."

The following two days were confusing for everyone. Granny gave the puppy name after name. She could not remember the puppy's name from one day to another! Mom Clay Horse knew this was not good for the dog. It would be hard for a confused dog to learn.

Granny asked, "May I call him Chuck or Charlie or Chad?"

"He is not a Chuck or Charlie or Chad, Mother," Miss Clay Horse protested. "You cannot call him any name you want. He needs to respond to one name. Besides, he is refined and very special. He must have a good name and he is my dog. You did not want him."

Mom Clay Horse reclined on her bed one evening. The little puppy sat at the edge of her bed. He stared at her. She stared at him. He seemed desperate to understand. "If only I could make human talk," he whimpered. "Give me a name. Call me something I would like to hear. I am a member of the family too."

Mom startled her puppy by sitting up abruptly. She blurted, "Mica! You are a clear, shiny piece of silica. You shall be a dignified Toy French Poodle. I will call you Mica Feldspar." She paused thoughtfully and chuckled, "You will be <u>Mister</u> Feldspar to Granny!" She laughed out loud.

The puppy had a name! He wagged his stubby tail. He ran to her and licked her face. He knew he was Mica. He liked his name very much. Mom playfully ruffled his silky coat. She teased him with his new name. She repeated, "Mica, Mica, Mica." He promptly learned his name. It was short and it had a nice sound.

Mica romped all over the bed. He wagged his puffy tail over and over. He liked his new name, not Chuck, not Charlie, not Chad, or any kind of horse! "I love my mom," he yawned. "I am my mom's Mica Feldspar!"

Mica tired of celebrating his new name. Miss Clay Horse said, "It is bedtime. Bedtime. It is time to sleep. Sleep. Shhh." He flopped on a pillow and quickly fell asleep. He appeared to be in a wonderful dream land. His tiny, pink eyelids twitched. He suckled his tongue. His short legs quivered. He was Mica Feldspar. All two and a half pounds of him was Mister Mica Feldspar.

Mica loved his new family. He dreamed of his mom throwing a toy for him to fetch. He dreamed of running outside with Mom watching him. He would run circles around her. "This is a wonderful adventure," he sighed.

However, the following morning was not so quiet. It began with a ruckus from Granny.

"You named him what?" Granny yelled. "You named him after a prophet in the Bible?"

"Mother," Mom Clay Horse responded, "You know about rocks and minerals. There is a difference between <u>Micah</u>, the minor prophet, and <u>Mica</u>, the rock. You did not listen to the 'feldspar.' He is Mica

Feldspar. He is a shiny little thing in our lives, Mom. He is here to give us love."

Granny was satisfied with the answer her daughter gave to her. Mica was a good name, a very good name. She could remember it. It was well with Granny.

Chapter 3

Playing with Granny

ranny rarely smiled, especially not at Mica. He tried to get her out of her grouchy mood. But how? Maybe she needed to play. He could be her friend. Maybe he could do something to make her chase and tug!

One day Mica darted out of Granny's bedroom with a slipper in his mouth. He ran and jumped on the couch. He laid the slipper down. He gazed down the hallway. Mica waited for Granny to come storming out of her bedroom. His cotton-ball tail shook furiously. He knew she would get

Granny's Slipper

her slipper and throw it so he could fetch it. It would be fun playing with Granny. Mica thought, "Granny will have fun playing with me. She will laugh like my mom!"

Just as Mica thought, Granny came out of her bedroom shortly. She shook her fist in the air. She yelled, "Mica, where is my slipper? I know you took my slipper!" Granny saw Mica sitting on the couch. She glimpsed at her slipper. She shook her fist again saying, "I knew you took it!" She scolded, "You took my stockings too. Where did you put them?" Not expecting an answer, Granny grabbed her slipper and returned to her bedroom.

Mica did not expect a grouchy Granny. She was supposed to play. Mom Clay Horse laughed silently as she overheard the commotion behind the kitchen wall. Mica was a happy puppy, maybe he was too happy. He did not understand adults may not want to play.

Mica Feldspar learned human language rapidly. He was the smartest dog Miss Clay Horse ever owned. Although he was only four months old, he knew words like 'play, toy, no, come here, up, down, chewy, bring, catch, go get it, bedtime, sleep, and many other words. Human language did not sound like mumbling anymore. He learned gestures and added them to words. He <u>could</u> understand. Some times no words were spoken. He understood hand gestures too.

Miss Clay Horse spoke to Mica throughout the day as though he were a child. Mica could tell by the tone of her voice if she was happy or not happy with him. If he made Granny upset, he knew it by the tone of her voice. He especially did not like time out in her closet. It was too much fun running around the house. Mom allowed him to run as much as he wanted, but not when he was naughty.

Miss Clay Horse remembered Granny had lost her tiny Chihuahua after she moved into her home. The house was located in wild, open country. She warned Granny many times to watch her puppy whenever it went for a walk outside. Granny, however, did not want to miss her television programs. Her little dog roamed outside alone.

Sadly, the dog left the yard. She was so small she went right through the fence. Granny did not put a collar on her dog so someone picked her up and gave her a new home.

Miss Clay Horse saw the Chihuahua several miles away one day when she was driving home from town. Miss Clay Horse did not tell Granny. The dog was inside a fenced yard. The new owner was watching her carefully and called her by a new name.

Miss Clay Horse did not want Mica to get lost. She always kept her little boy within her sight. His playground was inside the house. She stayed beside him whenever he went outside.

Miss Clay Horse loved Mica very much. She had to remember that Mica was a dog, not a boy.

Mom Clay Horse became upset whenever Granny shouted at Mica. Granny complained, "You scold me when I yell at Mica, but Mica gets away with everything!"

"Yelling is rude, Mother," Miss Clay Horse said. Of course, Mica was spoiled, but in a good and loving way. He was not a bad boy. She told Granny, "We give dogs a name to make them part of a family. They have little hearts and little brains that feel emotions. Their feelings get hurt. They want to love. They need to know they are loved. That is what makes a dog a man's best friend."

Granny huffed, "Well, he is <u>not</u> my best friend! He is not my friend at all. He plays tricks on me, like taking my slippers!"

Mica did not like Granny's suspicious looks. He tried to stay away from her but catching her off guard was so much fun! He sneaked into her room to see if there was anything he could carry away. He waited until Granny took a nap.

Mica knew that closed eyes meant 'sleep time.' That was how he settled for the night. Mom taught him to sleep by placing her hand over his eyes. She said, "Close those little blinkers. Sleep."

Mica peeked around Granny's bedroom door. He glimpsed at Granny's blinkers from time to time. He knew just when to strike. He would run away with whatever he could grab quickly. Granny did not know when Mica carried away with her things, not until she needed them.

Granny Sleeping

Z-Z-Z-Z-Z

One day Granny sped out of the laundry room asking, "Who took my slip from my laundry basket?" Mom Clay Horse did not answer. She went to her walk-in closet and found it next to Mica's pillow. Mica was sly. He knew when Granny was not looking.

There were times Mica did not sneak at all. He would go into her bedroom and wag his tail. Then he left quietly. One morning Granny finished making her bed. She sat on the edge of the bed to read a magazine. Mica decided on a friendly approach. He jumped on the bed to sit beside her. Granny stood up immediately. She shoved him off her bed. It frightened Mica. He felt threatened and growled.

Mom Clay Horse was busy in the living room when Granny ran to her. She yelled, "Your dog is vicious!"

This puzzled Miss Clay Horse. How could a small, playful puppy be vicious? She asked Granny, "Did Mica bite you, Mom?"

"No," she replied. "He growled at me!"

After hearing Granny's story Miss Clay Horse defended Mica. She reminded Granny it was best to train a dog; not to be cruel to it. "He growled because he was saying 'don't hurt me.' He was not going to bite you. I talk to him and he talks with me. He was talking to you."

Miss Clay Horse was patient with her mom. She continued, "You stand by the bed and point your finger to the floor. Tell him 'down.' A dog does not learn by being mean to him." She added, "God expects us to take care of animals."

No Bullying

Mica Says

No Bullying!

Mom picked up Mica gently. She scolded him.

"You have to leave Granny alone, Mr. Mica Feldspar. You cannot be a bully. That is not nice. No bullying!" Mica seemed to understand that bullying was not acceptable. It made too many people unhappy.

Mica quickly forgot the scolding. He went back to play with his toys. There was one <u>play thing</u> he did not like: that was the piano. If Mom played the piano, she could not play with a toy! He pushed a toy against her leg as she sat on the piano chair. If it did not get her attention, he looked for another toy. He pushed it against her leg again. There had to be a toy that would get Mom away from her piano. Mica wanted her to play with him, not the piano!

Miss Clay Horse decided Mica could play piano too. She sat him on her lap and placed his front paws on the keyboard. She pushed them gently on the keys. She pretended he was playing a song. Miss Clay Horse sang, "Jesus loves the little children."

Before she finished with "all the children of the world," Mica climbed onto the keyboard. He walked from one end of the piano to the other. He could play more notes that way. Mom hurried her singing, "black and yellow, red and white; they are precious in his sight. Jesus loves all the children of the world." That was the end of the piano lesson for Mica! He jumped back on Miss Clay Horse's lap.

Mica did not like the piano. He played to please Mom. Granny was not impressed with Mica's ability to play piano. She was upset with her daughter because she sang a church song to a dog!

Granny protested, "Dogs do not play piano and they do not go to church!"

Mica climbed back on the keyboard to show off to Granny. He teased her by walking from one end of the piano to the other one more time. The piano clanked and plunked. Mom laughed so hard she almost fell off the piano chair. Granny

Playing Piano

huffed and puffed back to her bedroom. She slammed her door.

Mica made his human mom happy. She laughed a lot. He loved to hear her laugh. Granny became more and more upset with Mister Mica Feldspar. She was not happy with her daughter or her dog. Granny argued, "You bought that dog for yourself. You never intended to give him to me!"

"God works in mysterious ways, Mom. I guess he planned for Mica to make me happy instead," Miss Clay Horse responded. "It was I who truly needed Mica." Miss Clay Horse added, "Mica is like a little rock that does not fade way. He is always there. He is always shining. Mica loves me even when I scold him. He lives to make me happy."

It was time for Granny to visit another daughter. The next house had no dog. She would be happy there. Mom Clay Horse packed Granny's things and drove her to the airport. When Granny's bedroom was vacant Mica jumped on her bed. He reclined on her pillow. He stretched and stretched as much as he could. He closed his tiny blinkers and rested. He liked the quiet time.

Chapter 4

A Day with Mica

Mica Feldspar did not always sleep at the foot of mom's bed at night. On cool nights he slipped under the blankets. Mornings were fantastic. They started new adventures. Every day was a special day for Mica.

Mica remained very still in bed until he saw Mom's blinkers begin to flicker. He gently crawled onto her chest to see if her eyes were staying open. He stared at her eyes. Sometimes Mom rolled over and slept a bit longer. Most mornings she said, "Yes, my blinkers are open!" Mica circled the bed wagging his puffy tail. He yapped at her. It seemed like he waited a very long time for her to wake up.

Mica jumped into his tub of toys. He tossed a toy here and a toy there. Finally, he found a favorite toy. He jumped back unto bed and shoved the toy against his mom. She giggled saying," Give me a chance to wash my face and brush my teeth, Mica!" He was in a big hurry to play every morning.

As Mom washed her face Mica jumped on the edge of the tub and onto the sink counter. He lapped the running water. "Mica," Miss Clay Horse said, "I need to rinse my toothbrush." He sat patiently watching every move she made.

Mica stood up. He sat down. He stood up again and sat down again. He let her know she was taking too long to clean up. Mica wanted to say, "It is my turn, my turn. Hurry! You need to clean me up before we play!"

"Okay, okay, young man," Mom Clay Horse remarked. "I will get your eyes and ears cleaned. I will brush your teeth as well." Mica did not like brushing his teeth. He allowed Mom to brush his teeth but not without a struggle. He clamped down on the toothbrush.

"Mica," his mom scolded, "Open your mouth. Let go!" She poked her finger into his mouth to release the toothbrush. He growled to let her know he was grumbling. He shook his head. He squirmed. Miss Clay Horse complained,

Brushing Teeth

Yuck!
Gr-r-r

"It says on this tube of dog toothpaste that you are supposed to like it!"

Mica was glad when brushing his teeth was over. Mom reached for Mica's hair brush. He loved his daily brushing. He especially loved a chewy. He received it as a reward for good behavior. Like a naughty boy, he was difficult to groom at times. He grew impatient if Mom needed to clip his hair. Poodles need special care and daily grooming.

Mica often thought, "Mom is using up my play time!" He squirmed and squirmed. She did not hurry and said, "Still, Mica. Stay still! STILL!" When Mom finished grooming him, Mica jumped off the counter and onto bed. He rolled and rolled on his fluffy blanket. Grooming made him feel very clean.

Miss Clay Horse smiled and commented, "You look so handsome. I bet you want a chewy!" Mica stopped rolling. A chewy? His ears perked up. He lived for a chewy! It was the next best thing to a toy! What a silly thing to ask every morning!

Mica knew where Mom kept his tasty morsels. He jumped off the bed and dashed to the pantry. When Mica received his reward he proudly paraded his chewy throughout the house. There was no one to watch the parade. It did not matter. It was his parade and he loved his chewy.

Mica ate his chewy while Mom fixed her breakfast. He was not allowed to bother her when she ate at the table reading her Bible. He sat by the sliding glass door in the dining room. He watched any activity happening outside. It was a good place to bask in the sun, too.

When Mica heard the clatter of dishes it meant Mom had finished eating. She was cleaning the kitchen. It was time for a toy. It was time to fetch. He ran to look for his toy. Mica dug into his toy tub again. He chose another favorite toy. He ran back to the kitchen to push it against Mom's leg.

Miss Clay Horse had arranged the furniture in the house so that Mica could have a clear runway from her bedroom to the den. It was a wonderful track for a small dog. This was Mica's time. She did not make him wait. She promptly began to throw the toy. "Go over there," she pointed to the other end of the house. He ran with great delight. "Get the toy," she shouted.

Miss Clay Horse had a painful right shoulder. It was difficult to throw toys for Mica. She threw toys with her left arm instead. Her aim was not good. Mica never knew which way his toy would go. At times a toy hit the ceiling fan. Other times it hit the walls. One time Mom broke a mirror! She laughed hysterically as she picked up the broken pieces and vacuumed the floor. They had a lot of fun.

Breaking Mirror

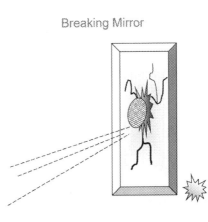

Fetching and catching continued until Mica no longer returned his toy. He grew tired and Mom was free to finish the rest of her chores. Mica kept an eye on Mom by following her from one room to another. He carried a doggy biscuit to chew as he waited for her chores to end.

Mica thought about lunch when chores were done. If his mom took a tray to the couch, she shared bits of her meal. If she sat at the table he would not get a thing. He watched to see if she would reach for a tray.

Yes! Mom picked up a tray. She took her meal to the living room. She asked Mica, "Where is your dish?" She turned the television on while Mica ran to the pantry. He fetched a plastic lid that served as a dish. Miss Clay Horse placed a small amount of food on his plastic plate. Mica knew he could not eat a full meal of human food. He could only taste it. He had to eat dog food to stay healthy.

Mica sat beside Mom on the couch with his plastic dish. He used his best manners. He sat still and waited for the next morsel. He was a perfect gentleman. Getting a little taste was better than tasting nothing. Mica loved tomatoes, potatoes, lettuce and anything else Mom ate. The morsels were also rewards for good behavior.

After lunch Mom stretched on the couch to read a book. Mica could not rest until she sat still. He made it his job to be with her wherever she went. He jumped on the sofa and napped by her feet. Miss Clay Horse often fell asleep with the book on her chest. When they awoke there were more things to do, like going to town.

Mica rode in the truck with Miss Clay Horse. At first he was strapped to the passenger seat. He was not permitted to sit on Mom's lap. He learned quickly. He could not sit behind the steering wheel. Mica could not be a distraction when she drove. Mom always thought about safety. Later Mica no longer needed to be strapped in. He slept quietly on the passenger seat until the truck stopped. If days were too hot or too cold, Mica stayed home.

Miss Clay Horse carried water for Mica whenever he rode with her. He never waited long. Once in a while she took him into a store where pets were allowed. He loved smelling everything and discovering new people. Best of all, he loved riding in a shopping cart.

At home, Mica continued fetching toys throughout the day. When Miss Clay Horse grew tired or her arm became too painful to throw, he dropped his toy. He ran several laps around the house, grabbed a toy, and squeaked his toy as he ran. One way or another, Mica had fun.

Bedtime was special. Miss Clay Horse talked about the day with Mica. He appeared to understand. His head tilted to one side and then the other. She burst into laughter. "We broke a mirror today, Mica! What a Mom you have! She cannot even throw a ball straight! My left arm is throwing better now, thanks to the exercise you give me."

Mica looked sadly at her. She petted him, "You did not break the mirror, baby. Mama broke the mirror. Come here, boy." She stroked his hair and smiled. "You are always a very good boy. Mama loves Mica." Mica licked her face. His fluffy tail wagged.

Miss Clay Horse spoke in few words for Mica to understand, "Mica good boy. No bad. Mica good. Love Mica." She yawned, "It was a very good day, a day with Mica Feldspar." Miss Clay Horse patted Mica's pillow and whispered, "It is bedtime, boy. Time to Sleep." She reached for the lamp and turned the light off. He fell asleep hearing his Mom say, "We had such a good day, a very good day with Mica Feldspar. You are my angel."

"Woof, Woof!"

THE END

What does Mica say about Bullies?

What does Mica say about bullies?

You cannot make friends by being mean. Bullies are mean because they want to feel big and important. Being mean hurts everyone. Teachers must take time away from teaching to correct a bully. That hurts the class because time is wasted.

If a bully picks on you, walk away. Do not pay attention to what he or she does. If a bully hits you, tell a teacher and your parent. Tell the Bully, "<u>Be nice</u>!" Everyone wants a bully to be nice.

Treat others the way you want them to treat you. Be polite. Let us all try to be nice - and more nice - and most nice!

Mica Feldspar

Printed in the United States
By Bookmasters